Oysterlight

Cheryl Pearson was born and raised in Cheshire, but now lives and works in Manchester. Her poems have appeared widely in journals and magazines including *Antiphon, Bare Fiction, Crannog, Neon, Envoi, Prole,* and *Southword.* She has also had work featured in anthologies produced by The Emma Press, The University of Chester Press, and Puppywolf Press. She won the High Sheriff's Cheshire Prize for Literature in 2016, and was nominated for a 2017 Pushcart Prize. When she isn't working or writing, you can find her drinking beer in the Peak District. *Oysterlight* is her first full-length collection.

Oysterlight

Cheryl Pearson

P_indrop Press

Published 2017 by
Pindrop Press
1 Oakwood Drive
Newton Mearns
Glasgow G77 5PU
UK

www.pindroppress.com

ISBN 978-0-9956805-4-8

A catalogue record for this book is available from the British Library.

Typeset by Pindrop Press (Palatino Linotype).

Printed and bound in the UK by Lightning Source.

Cover image by Sergiy Artsaba (Shutterstock).

Acknowledgements

Grateful acknowledgment is made to the editors of the following publications, in which some of these poems first appeared: *14 Magazine, Antiphon, Bare Fiction Magazine, Neon, Best of Manchester Poets 1, 2 & 3* (Puppywolf Press), *The Cheshire Prize Anthology* (University of Chester Press), *The Compass Magazine, Crannog, Driftwood Press, Envoi, Picaroon, QU Magazine, Skylark Review* (Little Lantern Press), *Slipstream Press, Southword, Tincture* and *When Women Waken*.

For Chris –

For everything. For always.

Contents

Mam Tor

That one tor, run through with bronze
and built on bones. A hundred centuries of the same sky

pouring into the same bowl. Where the grass runs like a river.
Where grudging sheep shit in steaming pats, and the heather

burns everywhere, hemming each green fold and loamy seam,
fed on old blood and wild air, wrapping its roots

in the earth-drowned hair of that settlement's daughters.
Whose ghosts are pressed in the print of our boots.

Where the light is pure and water-clear. Where once, we saw
a star blaze out of the world, a wake of flame at its back.

Where we strung our words in the dark to replace it.
Where *love* and *grace* now hang, like exclamation marks.

Pre-Dawn

Pre-dawn I wake, and your breathing finds me,
places me into this bed, this room, this
sudden not-quite-morning. You won't mind me
folding into your side, so I fold; kiss

the tangled mat of hair on your bent arm;
smell the yeasty smell which makes your skin taste
of wheat. Once, in Wales, we went to a farm
where a similar smell rose from the waste

of horses – a homely smell, redolent
of good earth, heat, sweat, physical labour.
I tucked myself into you, nonchalant.
Breathed you in as I do now, bed-neighbour

on this dark dawn, as the clock enforces
order and you dream – perhaps of horses.

How To Catch A Mermaid

With one breath, held till your lungs
burn like suns. So she sees the fire

in your face. Take a gift of Italian
lace. Like seafoam against the wet of her hair.

A throatful of earth words: your vowels
as round as the coins she teased

from the silt as a girl. Moons
she tested with tongue and teeth, tasting metal

and cleverness. Your arm next to hers,
skin full of skyshine. Gold beside

her sun-shy bleach. Perhaps she is tired of brine.
Give her sweet. Take her honey, sunk in a jar.

Or the wrecked feather you pulled
from a beach. She needs to know how worlds

can come together. How you both taste
of salt and rust underneath.

Daphne Considers An Alternative Outcome

You brought me water, listened to me talk.
The whole time, you were plotting like a crook:
my breasts in either hand, the trophy of my body lifted above
your equally golden body.

I thought you were wonderful, actually. I was thinking *love*,
when you were thinking *mine*. Like I was something you could take
and keep: a diamond, an acre, a milky sheet of silk.
And then you lunged, wearing that thief's look.
All sex and muscle, all bulk.

What else could I have done?
If I'd frozen then, I'd have died later.
Instead, I spun on a hot heel and ran.

Know this:

you could have worn this skin.
A glass of wine, some time.
I'd have turned myself into your open hands,
flowered in the bowl of your palms.

Not literally. Not like this green dress
I stepped into and became.

I mean the kind of flowering where the body is helpless
not to burst out of itself into brightness. The kind where I'd spill
into brilliant millionths. Bright petals against a bright sky.
Calling *yes* to you, calling your name.

Message

I let them go, that was the point of it. Prayers sealed into Merlot-
scented glass, love letters gathered like butterflies into jars
to undress printed wings on other continents. Or else to falter
feet away in the breakwater, never having breached another coast.
I loved the bulbed bottoms, glass so thick it killed the world.
Loved the way I knew my words were safe, those folded paper
ships with their cargo of language. No coffee. No steaming cattle
in the hold. Just words I could no longer keep.
I never saw a bottle twice: once they were gone, they were gone,
off to France, or Mexico, out to the far horizon's double-blue.
The odds are good that some sank, too –
a burp of bubbles, one last skyward glug, then down, for miles
of salt and silence, the notes inside released in undulating lace.
Scraps of pencilled prayers. Drowned cries. I let them go,
but sometimes at the table, even now, a fat cod will open its mouth
in surprise. *You, I know you.* And I meet myself
in the stilled silver of its eye.

Counting Stars

The smell of ice in the pines. Cold and green,
like lungfuls of mint. Your shoulderblades like angelwings
cleaving the grass. Moses parted water like that.
It wasn't as miraculous as this. Us. Your skin, the white of it shining
through cotton. You make a circle of thumb and finger,
a telescopic lens. You say, *Let's try and count the stars,* and I watch
as you sift the universe through to me, all that old assorted light
numbered, defined, falling through the bone ring like so much salt.
I know it now. How galaxies collapse.
How whole worlds can be born in a throat.

The Memory Of Water

The salt you left behind, came back without.
Aspirin-clouds. Lion-mouths. The flower. The root.

The bright cry of a christened head.
Every ankle on earth. Every wellington boot.

What it's like to make a rainbow.
(The moon).

What it's like to fall out of the world.
(The moon).

Whisky. River-weeds. Oil. Wine.
The blank swivel of a halibut's eye,

the freckled sunrise on the belly of a trout.
The taste of skin, that line from eye to throat.

Whether mermaids exist.
The peeling boards of a boat.

Shipwrecks. Sparrowbeaks.
(The moon).

Where all the pearls are.
All the drowned bones.

How the inside of a cloud tastes.
How it felt to be snow.

Joan Of Arc Waits For The Flames

They burned her horse first, made her watch
as they hustled his gleaming furniture into flame.
His tail, his mane, gone in a shock of sparks.
She hadn't known a horse could scream like that.
Hadn't known that pain came in layers, like an onion –
as one was stripped away, another, larger, moulded on the last,
gleamed underneath, brought burning water from her eyes.
When the fire reached his centre, she felt her own heart catch.
How soft then seemed the plates of her armour. How thin her skin,
through which grief flooded like sunlight through glass.
The thought of her own death, so close she could taste it –
fat-spit, lung-burn, sooted rib. Then out of her mind: the rope
of her Voice. *Think cold as the flames peel away from your bones.*
As her wrists were tied. As the torch-flame leaped. As her hems
and ankles lightened. *Think snowmelt. Think
stalactite. Think ice-storms. Think stone.*

Girl As Star

You may not realize this, but a girl
is in constant conflict with herself.
A girl is held together

by her own gravity.
Her properties may be determined

by observing her motion through space.
How bright she shines.

For at least a portion of her life,
a girl emits light. Some girls

are visible at night.

Gathering Evidence

Say it begins with *hairpin*. The sheets pulled tight as the alibi,
the clear pin in the centre. Your hair is red, not blonde.

His sudden taste for mints, the ghost of certain scents
that hang and cling at the edge of his jaw the way

sea-mist clings at the shore-line. Dead air
when you answer the phone. The crime scene hums.

Dust for lips as well as fingerprints,
comb for brassy hairs on cotton slips.

The evidence accumulates. Once, you saw a cut tree fall,
traced the trunk with a fingertip. Concentric circles

spool like this: each clue larger, louder, than the last,
each one confirming the one before, like an echo

confirming the first call. Say *guilty*. Say
undeniable. Say *cliché*.

The slim pin at the storm's still centre.
Tipped plastic, clear as water. Clear as day.

The Shape Of Things

Where sails fill and swell with the salt air,
sparrows once settled paper-thin bones
and sent clear notes to the sky like prayers.

Now ankles flash where eggs rested,
the colour of breath on winter mornings.
Just as fragile. To touch one meant

to alter a life: the mother beaked
the touched ones from the nest.
How many little deaths. How many ghosts

sing here in the ship's ribs? The rum matures
like they could never, belted into barrels
where squirrels ran on gymnast feet

and dapper magpies rattled off their shots.
Who knows what teenaged names lived here before,
what blade-commemorated loves were cut,

and scored, and cut again. Where pigeons rolled
their purrs. Where doves bent sweetly
to each others' necks. We trace the pool

and warp of currents in the grain,
the very shape of water held there like a proof.
Like evidence. *Everything must change.*

Interview With An Angel, After The Fall

What was it like?
I imagine like falling in love – an exhilarating terror,

in which everything came glass-clear,
in which everything was suddenly dangerous.

I am a creature constructed entirely of love,
but I have no heart. Even still, I'd swear

I felt it beat the whole way down
with bone-breaking rhythm.

How did I feel when my wings fell away?
Like a fish pulled bloodily from its element.

I hung between stars, once, rowed the light home.
Then I fell, and the sky let me go,

the breath of God
still hot on the back of my neck.

How does it feel to be human, at last?
Like thunder being born.

Like a new lamb trying, and failing,
to find its legs.

The Reality Is Always Different

You'd have written it differently – gothic romantic,
fans of hair and braids of weed, slow-billowing skirts.
White palms up like cups of sunny water.
The fact is you thought she was litter, at first.
Someone's fly-tipped crap. You held that
through the looping blue of police car lights,
the hours of hard chairs and official signatures.
You told yourself dead fish, plastic sack.
She didn't become a woman till a few days later,
your yolks cooling to gold stones on the plate.
Her grainy anyone-eyes staring out from the paper.

Four Moons

First moon

The sky's colour at this hour
as it closes on itself like a sleeping flower.
The garden, golden in the light, now blue,
and strung with lanterns, paper moons.
You smell of woodsmoke, taste of wine.
Your fingers chart the constellations of my spine.

Second Moon

You speak to me of lovers who left.
Your voice is the night train,
rattling the dark.

Third Moon

The ponds are sealed, the moon's
preserved in ice.
White moth pressed
under glass.

The water's been brought
to a full stop.
In the dark,

the fish make semi-colons;
dot, dash, dot, dash.

Fourth Moon

The world - has it broken open?
The night - has it cracked?
The clouds hurl the heat, they are furious.
Our sweat boils and evaporates.
What is this, is this the end?
Is that the four horsemen, trampling the roof?

Medusa

Once, I was golden, and lifted like a trophy.
Once, my body made men howl.

These days, I'm worse than invisible. Just a
rusting voice, a fabulous crown.

To pass the time, I talk to my statues.
Pretend them back to handsome, use

a flirty tone. Sometimes I take off all my clothes -
despite the cold - and pose,

naked, on a bent stone knee. Or fill
the chilly curl of a fist with my breast.

Once, just once, I toppled one and cracked
him open like an egg. Combed through concrete ribs

to find the rock that was his heart. And then I broke it.
See, I told him, *how you like it.*

Selkie Poem

Their golden bodies stepped from their seal bodies.
Stretched from rock to sky, the split slicks
of their seal-cauls gaping behind them:
a hundred smiles, a hundred gleaming exits.

I longed to peel out of my body like them.
Heel to skull in the pale curls of one skinning.
I wanted to stamp the rocks with my secret feet,
put the print of my new self on the earth

while my cast pelt baked and stiffened.
Eventually salt and heat would seal it.
And I would be dry and clothed differently.
Somewhere else, in a different world.

The Cartographer's Daughter

He brought the world to the kitchen table –
unceremonious, a small square he lifted out of itself,
two wings beating away from that centre crease.
Again, it opened, and again, like a wild goose breaking out of winter,
chasing light. Until all seven continents replaced
the knuckled oak, my mother's plates,
an ocean in place of water glasses, cups.
How we travelled, fingertip by fingertip. I rubbed the deserts thin
with my camel hands. He obliterated France with his thumbs. Once,
he drew two dragons over Spain at my request, red and rearing,
barking flames. I learned history from his knee, I learned geography.
I learned that there are maps which are not paper maps,
but exist in the body, its seas of blood, and lines of memory.
The word *childhood*, and I am back: those golden afternoons
with my father, a pan of milk rolling to a boil, and the fine net
of latitudes and longitudes, the flat blue box of oceans, bitten coasts.
When he died, I knew to map my grief, that naming it would keep me
found. I brought out the old square, brown and thin
as onionskin, and let its dry wings open. *An adoration
of mountains*, I thought. *An inheritance of snow.*
I held my new daughter, blood of my blood, blood of his.
Hushed her curdling cries until she calmed. There,
when she stilled, and smiled: the lines of his face, a map
going all the way back to the stars.

Whitby Harbour

The harbour gives us everything twice.
Brightly-doubled hulls and kissing masts.
The abbey, warm as allspice in the sun.

Foot to foot, our mirror selves in wet sand
packed with light. A second sky
pearling our soles. Slow clouds.

The local cod parts for the fork as water
parts for the rock. The weedy wash
of the harbour wall. You pull a bone, thin as a hair,

from wrecked batter. Thin as the prayers
I cast like fishing lines out to the dark, where
slender hooks catch far, or else are sunk in ceilings.

Above us, at the town's peak, the ghost
of a different fish makes its home – a whalebone
pitched like a tuning fork, bleached

by a dry world. Its double hums in a puddle
of salt. The old songs from ribbed halls.
The hymns risen from deep blue altars.

Bluebells

Out from under the wide sky, dim as dusk,
a settling. The floor weaves green, weaves gold,
the ceiling's leaf and light. Then
there! – a flood of sky in the under-wood,
thousands of cloudless blues on strings.
Wait for a wind to play them. Wait for them to ring –
the struck note, the blown flute, the song that sings
of the love in their wild throats, the love in their blue roots,
the love for the wild colour and wonder of all things.

Oyster Boat, New York City

Remember how the boat stole our sense of balance?
We rocked and laughed on our heels like drunks
as the city shrank to a far blue line. My shoulders took the sun
and held it, two tipped cups of pink. You took my face
and held it, two palms and a kiss. There were years before you;
they too are blue and far away. It seems impossible, now.
That once my skin was clean of your prints. That once my name
was just a name, and not a bell rung in your mouth's dark.
We bought a dozen oysters, trembling in their shells.
Remember how they tasted, of colours and salt? That pearly wash
at the back of the throat. And love rising like a tidemark
in my body. Your body. I remember it exactly. How it felt to float.

Bat

Thin wing-spokes turned inside out,
a flimsy umbrella in high wind.
Just last night I saw, flickering about,
three, four, hitching star to star with sound,

casting ripples round the moon like stones
skipped across a pond. Now there's this: stiff in the grass,
alien. Examine the fine fan of bones,
fox-ears, fur. Look at its fixed, curdled face,

see your own occur in it. Palmed, it's dry
and cool as leather. Little sky-mouse.
Moth-mouthed predator. A vacant space high
in the roof, a tenant less in the house –

say a prayer for its small life. Say a spell.
Incant its names: Grey. Vampire. Pipistrelle.

Herman

You named him Herman: the yellow-striped brute
who'd spun his quarters on your kitchen sill. Most people
would have turned him out.
You let him claim that bit of corner
like a tenant, blotting out the knot of sky

beneath the gutter. At night he made
an eight-legged hole in the stars. I didn't get too close,
just cast him wary looks from the door while you
made tea, rinsed glasses, poured the wine. Decanted yolks
one-handed, shell to shell.

That was June. I didn't know I loved you yet,
but thought I might.
Those golden weeks of beers and firsts went on for years.
We learned the worst things last, as lovers do.
(I knew by then, for sure. I knew).

The belted waist, the eyes that saw six worlds at once.
He sat like a struck note at the centre of his strings.
You brought me, in January, the tiny husk.
Said, *No flies for months. He must have starved, poor thing.*
He looked as light as breath there in your hand: it hurt my throat.

My eyes were salt. *So sensitive,* you smiled.
It wasn't even about the spider.

Orpheus And Eurydice

The cool gloom of the underearth. The
watched spot, top of the spine,

hot as a target's centre. Look: to miss
the hissing line of parting grass –

it could have happened to anyone. To try to suck
the sickness from a struck heel, after –

that was love. Her red foot
in your hand, her death snagged

in your teeth. You'd flout
each natural law to bring that mouth

back to your mouth. To move beneath
her again like a river. And so you chance the stranger

in the dark: the handful of notes, the barter,
then the double-tap of footsteps

in your wake. Look back, and you lose her
forever to silence; a roiling ceiling

of worm and root. And so you move.
And so you move. Until you see that faint first light

and hear her draw in breath – or think you do –
and turn. To a whirl of skirt, a flash

of bloody foot. There, then not.
For the rest of your life, she'll be the obstacle

you cannot pass. More real than if you'd led her back
to clouds, and food, and flesh. You know

what death is now. This life without.
You know the dead weight of regret.

Out Of Water

How flash-quick that vital line was breached,
how sudden the drowning in sky –

the banked fish gasped as though crying out
for the stippled riverbed, the lost underlight;

choked on throatfuls of sun. The eye
dragging clouds into its rolling pivot,

like fairground candyfloss catching
the stick. I saw none of it,

but I saw it all. Next milky morning, the gold dog
rooting. She came when I called,

her thrilled nose starred with the leavings.
Could she scent the striped light in which

the fish hung before leaping? The breath
of the bird as it stripped the wreck

back to the rungs? I wonder if afterlives
swing from an owl-mouth's ceiling,

the way my own bones
close over waterless lungs.

Poem Written While You Sleep

I walk the cold floors of your body
carefully –
the cold floors
like museum floors, full of bones.

Sound reverberates, the smallest word
courts an echo.
I alone
can walk these halls of white,
can delicately step
and settle where I choose –

I am light as a snowflake
settling on water.

River

Closes over coins and broken trolleys.
Sucks the boots from feet and rattles

mouse bones like dice in a cup.
Works and works, supple as a muscle.

Eats light, heat, animal,
accepts any tossed offering as fuel.

Licks sheep skulls clean of memory,
stashes unpopular treasure

in each tributary – condoms
slow as jellyfish, cans

stamped flat, the occasional unlucky pet.
Green in winter, gold in summer,

it gleams and raves. Weaves
over stones the sky will never touch,

braids itself, unbraids itself,
moves like a dancer.

Claims anything it can:
clouds, and keys; first diamonds, last prayers.

The Bearded Lady

The boss man parts the curtains like he parts his hair –
with confidence and grease. *One night only!* the posters scream
in the same red as the silk pegged to the field,
where flattened grass knows dim for the first time; knows hush.
But back here, past the sawdust circle, the hooves
are far as thunder; the sequins stars in another universe.
Here, in the quartered dark, the curtain falls behind you like water,
and your throat rehearses every swallow twice.

This is how you know she's real: the sour tang
of booze on her breath, the fur of her bangled arm. All night
she sits and soaks up looks like this. All night she stares from under brows
that might hide wolves or bloodied children, her stiff chin eating light.
You've seen a mile of wheat do that – take sunshine down like a pint
of beer, then spill it back to gild the sky, all gold, all joy.
Nothing comes back from that midnight glare, the bib of whiskers
hung from ear to jaw and boiling with shadow. She collects your minute
there with the rest. And, when you leave, the sharp scent of your sweat.

In tens of years, a grandchild dandled from your lap will hear
how witchcraft shimmered in the dark that night, a haze of heat.
You will never know her only thought was if she would ever get
to taste, firsthand, a kiss. Whether it would be salt or sweet.

Oyster

An oyster is not beautiful. It has no face. It sits
on its bed of rock or ice

inanimate as stone. A hard purse
shut by a calcium clasp,

perhaps a compact, blind as
a closed eye, glass

reflecting only darkness.
Prise it open, scoop it from the basin

of its own nacreous shell.
It gilled in salt, once, swallowed the gels

of brine and plankton. Held itself close
to make hard, marvellous colour. Tell

me you don't feel anything at all
as you swallow the unpearl, the quiver.

Blue Moon

No cowl tonight, no monk's hood.
Just her face, full blast. A shock as bright as a struck cheek,
a branch snapped in full silence. A break like a fault-line
crazing its way along a frozen creek.

Call it a second coming: she's back,
ringing and ringing, the way the truth
rings after the lie has been discovered, and everything you've known
comes cold and clear. You don't have the words.
She's like. She's like.
A broken wrist with its hub of bone.
A pearl. A stone. A tossed coin. The thin note
singing from rimmed glass.

See how luminous? See how wide?
She is the owl's eye, full of kills,
stars at her feet like old skulls. She has eaten the dark.
A hundred deer simmer under her.
Bats shriek in the park.

Dam Swimming

Before I found the dam, I swam in rivers. Weeds streaming
behind me like ribbons, a green rime on my skin.
The water here is different. There is no mineral echo, no clear taste,
but a human print on it, unmistakable – the slick of soap
rinsed from the skin of swimmers, the tang of rust
from the broken bikes and buckling trolleys in the shallows.
This water will never end in wildness, or break in foaming rolls of salt.
This water is quiet, and well-known. Even the steeple at the bottom
is on record; the cottages where only fish drift, now,
where steam once rose from cups, and coals were banked to a glow.
Each time I swim here, I go deeper, but never deep enough
to bruise my feet on roofs, or move through the old school's silent hall
like a shark cruising a wreck. Always the human need for air,
the quick shot up for brightness and breath. Always, the brightness
is deafening, always that first breath tastes cold, and green,
as though a forest had grown in my throat while I was under,
the way seeds flower with darkness, and water. I scull the dancing net
of light, imagine birds pouring forth from my mouth,
while underneath, long pike glide where sky once hung;
new silver where the old bell rang.

Jellyfish

It sits on the sand like an alien parcel,
wrapped in rubberwater, waiting for collection.

No ribbon, but its innards loop and gleam
like strings of tinsel. A gull or crustacean

has tried its luck - here and there are dips pecked in
by scrapping beak or claw, a constellation

of hungermarks denting the inedible.
The thing stinks – the tin reek

of metal held too long in a sweating palm,
of wet sand, seaweed, rot. We hold our breath,

crouch for a closer look but do not poke
with sticks as some have done,

or counter the tremors
slammed through sand by placing stones.

Perhaps a heart attack looks like this,
a bright sprawl of pain in a stricken muscle.

Or a children's maze, the exit
traced in a muddle of crayon.

There's nothing to be done for it, now.
We leave it, shelved on the flattened castle

a child built and the tide will cancel.
It will go, too.

Despite its looks,
it is nothing special.

All The Things We Cannot Keep

Plum jam in the mornings, knees bruised from days spent out,
and far - bike flying to the thin line of the horizon and – brake! –
the streak of her hair like the tail of a star. Her patched basket
fills and brims: parchment-paper leaves gone bronze,
dried frogs pressed centimetre-thin by cars.
Once, a moth with eyes for wings left silver ash on her palm,
a graphite smudge she held close but apart, not wanting it
to disappear. (*I am here*, she marvelled; *I am here*). Evenings, the bathwater
runs out grey. Foam and steam, the grubby scrim of her down
the drain. In bed, she dreams of pipes that bend and flex to the sea.
Of fishes waiting open-mouthed to be fed by what she gives them:
cell of mothdust, rug-flat frog. Cell of knee-skin, and gold tree-leavings
lifted from the park. She wants to live forever. She wants
the world. This is what she knows: nothing's hers to keep. Not even
her own bones. And so she parcels herself
out in sleep. Sifts herself out to the waiting dark.

You ask if I choose a shape when I become a cloud

The truth is, I let the light decide.
There's a surrender in rising that's almost holy.
The photons asking things of my body,
my body replying: Yes. *Make of me*
herringbones, braided ropes, a ladder. Make me
a bank of snow, a hand of fire.
Once, I was a lion with the sun on my tongue.
Once, a ship sailing over the sea, slow
and smooth as the blue whales under me.

It's hard to come back to earth
when you've given birth to rain. To assume again
breasts and the old familiar attitudes
when you have tasted mountains, and moons.
Since you ask, my favourite shape
was the horseshoe. It may have been a fluke,
but I was found by a storm, as if I had drawn it just by becoming.
A magnet hauling a line of filings. Just thinking about it –
the static, the smelted metal, the flash –
makes gooseflesh rise on my grounded skin.
To feel that electric again. That known.

Train Poem

The miles unravel between two lines
thinned to a single distant point.
Miles of clouds trying to keep pace,
miles of hollyhocks blurred
to a stuttering purple.
You watch me from the window
watching you back in the glass.
We pass a yellow train, whose carriages I first
mistake for rape or wheat, split-second sunshine
at the corner of my eye. This time, which is time
out of itself. When we are smeared for an hour
between two geographies. No past. No home.
Just this. The quiet hum of us pulled
from place to place. The thin hiss of the brakes.
The jump and clatter of the track. Now
a ribbon of brick. Now
a field of sheep, whisked off in a flash like
a magic trick. And now the grey salt-smelling sea,
far off, but coming. Coming. Yes.

Bluebeard

The first time I saw him, I cried.
That beard he had, it made his face look like the ocean,
or the sky with its constellations put out.
He said *bride*, I heard *blood*. But I had no choice.
We rode off into the cold night, and just like that –
I was someone's wife.

He was gentle as it happens. He softened himself for me.
His hands memorised my body
so he knew exactly when and where to touch.
He sent his men for my favourite foods – peaches, smoked cheese,
butterscotch – and dressed me in diamond brooches,
strings of pearls.

I couldn't believe my luck!
Of course I'd heard the rumours. His previous wives, a horde of them,
all gone. Swallowed up like echoes, like stones closed over by water.
Some said nineteen. Others, ninety.
He told me, lightly, that people love their stories.
Printed me with kisses like the seal on a guarantee.

Six months passed like this.
A blur of peacock-coloured silks and Chinese fans,
of good champagne and gemstones on my hands,
of swimming like wild salmon in the sheets at night.

I might have known it was too good to be true.
I will be gone for one night, he told me over breakfast.
It was June. I remember the clear light
and the oranges glowing like suns in their bowl.
(Blood oranges. That would haunt me later).

I must trust you, my darling, with these.
My palm closed over a bracelet of keys.

Lock every window and door before bed. My heart. My treasure.
I ask only this: that you never, not for anything,
go to the rooms in my tower.

I promised, waved him off, blew kisses from the door.
And then I stewed.

All day I sat and thought.
I felt like Eve or Pandora:
apple, box, bolted rooms, the one thing I knew I mustn't do
the only thing I wanted to.
I sat outside the door for hours, the keys burning my wrist.
I sat there so long my spine bruised from the wood.

My sister visited, brought me wine.
Gossiped like a bird in my ear:

What if his other women are in there?
Oily, naked, playing themselves like instruments,
smiling like foxes waiting for his return?
What if he loves them
more than he loves you?

I could make an excuse –
the truth is I listened because I wanted a reason.

Looking back, it's the colour I remember most.
The terrible red on the floor, the walls,
the red on my palms and my slippers,
the indelible red on the key in the door.
The women on hooks were almost incidental,
hanging there like a question
repeated and repeated:

Who's there? Who are you? What do you know?

Seals, San Francisco

I love the seals immediately. Fat
and wet on their special pier, gleaming
like mirrors in the June sun. The wood slats
ripple with their corpulent teeming

as if the pier itself had come alive,
muscular, sturdy, rimed with salt. Awkward
out of their element, in it they dive
and flash with fishlike grace, transported

in the cathedral quiet of those depths
to sleek precision, all elegance
and poise: ballerinas dance their steps
with that same clean magnificence,

make of their bodies those same shining knives.
Up here, the seals are stunned by gravity.
They pitch and roll like sweet-natured drunks surprised
by their sudden, shambling instability.

One sports the bracelet of a recent bite.
Perhaps a shark; they cruise here, thin and mean,
waiting for swimmers to kick an invite,
stitching the bay with their glittering seams.

Or another bull, maybe; quick to fight
in the summer heat. Their slick skins crawl
with shivering nets of liquid light.
A cargo of marvels. An angel's haul.

They could be survivors from the ribs of a wreck.
Or selkies, forced by genetic blip
to return after a time to those wet pelts
and pull them back up over golden hips,

leaving behind for their brooding lovers
only their templates on a cooling sheet.
A faint salt scent in the cotton covers
that the first bitter laundering will delete.

Heptonstall Churchyard

Scrubbed stones gleam in the late sun. Gilt lettering,
coloured cellophane, roses crisped to a dark mottling.

Stuffed bears, faintly-mildewed, solemn-eyed, guard the graves
of children. Across the yard, a ginger cat goes stiff

at our intrusion, shoots disdainful yellow looks
our way, flashes us the pursed star of his behind. Dismissed,

we comb the rows of indexed stones, dead names
making temporary homes in our mouths. Ten minutes in,

I find her name and stop, mid-step. Damp-palmed,
abruptly sweaty. A lip of pebbles neatly rims her pitch,

a bush of something wild describes the patch
above her breast. Two baskets by her feet are brown

with drying posies, and a pair of clay goddesses
squat above her name, fierce-faced, stoutly female.

I left the tulips in the service station. Picked instead
a snatch of heather to tangle with tribute and weed. She wanted

her bones to whiten among it. A wood pigeon calls from the trees,
a hollow sound. *Who? Who?* I give her name in answer.

Laika

Stars carved by the ship.
Air carved by the dog's swim.

Once I saw a friend pull a trout from the water,
a thin ribbon of muscle that lashed

against and against the inevitable. Until
it stilled. Looked death in the eye.

That's how I imagine Laika
looked at the last. Out of her element,

eyes travelling like old light
back to the past.

Rumpelstiltskin

Light slants through
the blinds in our bedroom, turning the hairs
on your arms to gold.

Gently, I wind their gilded wires
through my fingers.
I am careful. I am slow.
Your sleep-heavy breathing marks time.

I wind. I wind. I lift your hair
to the light and hold it,
watch it turn
from brown to gold.

I am an alchemist
measuring my treasure,
one brilliant strand against another.

Your body, slatted with light,
the riches of your skin –
I hoard each minute you sleep
with a miser's pleasure.

The day we saw a rabbit, dead in the canal

We thought it was a bag, at first. A square
of fur, lazily turning in the slow water. Half-sunk,
the heft of it pulling it under. Then it turned towards us,
and we saw its eyes - blind, milky, rolled back to the whites,
as though, like a yogi, it had spurned the world to better
navigate the lights of its own mind. Oblivious
to the streak of green canal, the yellow
blaze of October leaves. The one knot
of our cold hands, and the human smell of us,
from which, before, it would have bucked
and leapt. Then the water shifted,
and the shock of its jaw shone out like the moon.
The jolt of that sight, the secrets under skin.
The bold alliance of air and skull, the dereliction
of the thing, in whose wrecked face we couldn't help but see
our own eventual dismantling.

The Water Dowser

Running through generations like a river, alongside
the gene for red hair, and the family name: this gift
of summoning the earth's weather. *A humming*

in the wrists, is how he describes it. I picture his hands,
like knuckles of ginger, thrumming with bees: tiny harbingers
browsing his tributaries, raising the alarm

in the hand/arm hinge. In the old days, they called it
witching the water; walked their switch of hazel, switch of willow,
waiting for the dip and twitch that meant they'd struck gold,

and clear-running cold would follow. Years ago, a palmist
on a seaside pier winnowed a future from the forks of my hands.
I believed in magic. Now, I stand in a dry field watching

a man draw water like doves from his sleeves.
He tells me, *Some people don't trust this*, spits, then grins.
I think of moons. Salt lines in the sand. My blood

going out,

coming in.

Summer, Early Evening

I sit in a fan of shadow under the pines,
book half-read, spine-up in the grass,
a glass of wine sweating in my hand. The starlings
are spilling their gladness into the deep blue hour.
The sky has begun to copy the maps from their breasts:
first one star, then another, glittering duplicates that double
and redouble as the dark deepens, as the garden settles and rests.
The roses close in on themselves, flushed and quiet
as sleeping children. The pigeons still in the cool bowls of their nests.
I saw a fox once detach itself from these shadows,
a flame peeling off from a fire. A ribbon of colour
unravelling in the gloom. I watched through the blinds as he tested
the air like a sommelier. Could almost share the world he found there –
bouquet of mouse and frost, undertones of earth,
afternotes of cloud and star.

Anchoress

That one heart, in the dark, at the centre.
A bloodship breasting the blind miles towards God.

She imagines the villagers' prayers are like fish.
Imagines her chest, full of nets. Sometimes, she thinks

her skin gives off light from the heat of all those burning pleases.
The sorries, flaming in. The smoking regrets.

All the lives cast onto her breath. The wives
who throw crucified shapes in the sheets, but whose blood

still comes in with the moon. The men with dry fields,
and small mouths in their houses. The girls who are green,

sick with love, or without it. They flood her skull, drown
the things that might otherwise rise in the wash before sleep:

stars and rain in the slow surf of her. Gold sunskin.
White moonskin. Her onceupon undersky shine.

Only prayers stay afloat in the black room - she has lost
her father's voice, her mother's face. She herself is weighted down

by the words she holds, one in each hand like a stone.
In the left, she holds *anchor*. In the right, she keeps *grace*.

Penelope

Dignified, you weave your decadent shroud,
embroidering each stitch with queenly calm.
You will not be touched; each new prince or king
is warned: *Leave her be. You must let her grieve*
first. Let her finish weaving. Let her thread
spell out her sadness – ring her hand with gold

after. You know full well they want your gold,
your breasts in either hand, your crown. The shroud,
if all goes well, will best their greed; the thread
you stitch so tight by day unpicked by calm,
determined hands each night. And so you grieve,
grieve, braiding out your sorrow for the king

your heart is slyly sure still lives, the king
ingested years ago by the warm, gold
mouth of the horizon. How long you grieve
in peace depends on your performance: shroud
your cunning, keep your head, think only calm
thoughts. Steady any trembles with your thread.

You keep a little of each scene you thread
to hush the queries you pre-empt: *the king*
has been gone how long? Still she sews? Bent, calm
at your work, the patterns gild your knee, gold
lattice, lace, gilt tapestry – all shroud
the anxious tapping of your feet. You'd grieve

for years, but fear you lack the nerve to grieve
forever. They drink your husband's wine, thread
his gems at their throats, claim the beds and shroud
their shoulders in his furs. *When I am King –*
you hear their boasts and dream of murder. Gold
blade through the breast. Death in short order. Calm

in the palace… No. Breathe. Will yourself calm.
Your husband will return and they will grieve
each slur, each smutty look, each joke. The gold

60

band of your wedding ring gleams as you thread.
Spelled to pig by witch, or ash by death... no king
of yours would go so readily. The shroud

unfolds in your calm, capable hands. Thread
picked. Stitched. Picked. Stitched. *I will not grieve. My king
is not dead.* Gold eyes fixed fast on the shroud.

Love Poem For A Broken World

If shoots could be cut from the sun and planted
in quiet rows, roots frizzing underneath, electric,
I'd stun the ground with hot seedlings.

Imagine: above, the wet slate returning
the same grey skies, then underfoot, a flood of sun,
rising in secret, rising, rising.

All winter, your feet would be strangely warm.
And then one morning, the blinds would open
on a changed world – brilliant streets,

and brilliant people filling them, blinking
back light. Stopping to bend and smell the miracle,
every ankle bright with sky.

Grizzly

I saw her catching salmon in July – fat hammers that gleamed and beat
against the river where she waited, still as a boulder. Ankle-deep.
Until that one fish hooked her eye, and she leaped –

the great fur heft of her crashing like a planet from the clear sky
to stun against the rock that smaller star. I watched as fish after fish
went dark, a book of matches struck and snuffed. One by one,

light by light. Later, I would see their radiance again:
death brightening each tooth, the way skulls might brighten
a hunter's belt – fishscales, shining in her mouth like a brace.

I would see the fish in her belly, dimmed, stripped.
Her mouth lit with trophies from their last, lost race.

On First Looking Into The Gorgon's Face

It's the beauty that shocks you, breaking apart
what you thought you knew, like a rock breaking ice
through to bright, cold water. The eyes are gold, the pupils
pits to fall into. A stare like a solar eclipse –
the black full stop, then the flare rising, a crown of spiking fire.

But her crown hisses and strikes. And by the time you realise,
you're already done for – fixed in a dream, language cooling
on the stone slab of your tongue. Her red
lips bless your throat. All those wild words you had. Now
you cannot even tell her *Yes*.

Insurance Policy

Let my blood run backwards twenty-four months
to the source of this, the source of us. My salmon-cells leaping
back to the dark. Let my heart collapse softly
on the sack of itself, a balloon expelling you
breath by breath. Let my neck forget the syllables you left
with tongue and teeth; let my hands unlearn *held*
and remember *release*. Let my bones come loose
from the shape tucked into the sheets at night,
let the moon print newly minted light along my spine.
Let me rock shut like an oyster over the pearl
of what this has become. Which is everything. The world
I cannot conceive of losing. Let me go back further, just in case.
Stars, carbon. A universe of blank space.

Statues With Fig Leaves

There was nothing gentle about bringing them
from marble. Each patient face was beaten
from stone, each milky muscle
wrought of sweat, brute force, and thunder. The biceps
bunched in curls, the rocky quads –
they do not look like surrender, but this
is the look of solid matter that has given itself
up to hammer, air, intent.

It's the hulk that shocks, the risen size
of the god, the boy. The blind eyes closed
on white, and the fig on the private crease
between mountainous thighs. Adam. Eve.
Original sin. Put your thumb on the spot
where the motif fails. The devil, they say,
is in the details.

Beachcombers

The winter sun hits wet sand,
and the struck world whitens.

The sea is lightning
strung with salt. The sand is cold fire.

You find a crab and lift it,
red legs clicking like worked locks.

You find a seahorse, crispbrown
and snappable, curled in a

permanent question.
But it's my find you handle like real treasure –

the mussel shell, hinged like a fairy-door,
with its tin stink and violet folds,

the insides holding their own wash of light
like a net of pearls cast at a throat.

I watch as you tilt your palm sunward,
then away, to see the lilacs rise,

to see the goldpinks shift. Your eyes
are crucibles where magic lives –

colours from nowhere, rainbows
rinsed from dead shell. I shift, too,

when you look at me like that.
I too am beautiful.

Things That Can Be Broken

The road's back, under boots and drills.
A bad tooth on a peach-pit.
Silences. Mornings. Sleeping-spells.
Stars shivered up in a kicked bucket.

A sick fingernail, ridged with infection.
Mirrors, and windows. A weak lock.
Sandcastle-keeps when the sea returns.
The braid of a fish-spine on a cutting block.

A Christmas wishbone in a pincer-grip.
A voice under fathoms of bad news.
A soft, dropped apple, coughing its pips.
A slow snail under careless shoes.

A fast. A heart. A sapling split
by axes, lightning, rot, disease.
A talcumed grandmother's chalky hip.
Ice under boot-heels in a winter freeze.

A confidence. A promise. A fever. A skull.
A jilted bride, glittering like dew.
A horse's leg on a difficult hurdle.
Bread, and circles. Me. You.

Deer On The Rise

As if the wood had moved
through Shakespeare's Scotland to finish here,
branches staggered on the rise and coming
closer, closer, until the armature of their bodies
becomes clear. Becomes thicker
than the mist that kept them shy
as brides behind their veils , and we see them as they are –
monarchs of the valley, the fabulous rigging
of their brown crowns scoring the sky.

That bristling along the sky's fault:
a gift we could not have imagined this morning
over ordinary eggs. Astonished,
we tread our breath so the spell holds,
our frozen shadows thin, unfabulous. How long
can we test the edge of the known world?
Listen, in the silence: praise rising
like a song from the grass. More beautiful
because we know it cannot last.

Persephone

Bulbs stud the ceiling.
I act like they are stars or birds.

I lie beneath
with the literal

weight of the world
above me.

I do not wrinkle in the dark.
I never look sad or sour.

Down here, our hands do the talking.
A message spelled into a palm,

a poem over breasts.
You move your hands,

make light, make heat.
I open and close like a flower.

Sister Grimm

A girl turned into a wolf that night.
Moon on her breath like old milk, tongues of light
on her shoulders. Legs, four of them now.
And stars of rain
strung in her fur.

Ask her what she wants –
it's all any girl wants.

Freedom, her own bones,
the wild air.

Ask what she has.

A dream rusting
in the back of her throat.
Yellow eyes, a bloodlust that parts
her hair
with its force.

Lot's Wife Looks Back

The sand shifts. The grass drowns in it.
I've seen a thousand camels drop and rot
to their struts. Ships of hoof and hair,
ships of star-torched throats. Their ribs
make churches for desert birds, which rise
like prayers in the cool bone halls.

Nothing is different. Everything's the same.
The glazed days bake like pots in a kiln.
A dropped pot can break. A heart. But not a curse.

How many suns, now. How many moons.

A woman, I said, *can step out of a dress. A bath.*
A room. She cannot step out of a life.

The hot sting of salt in a cut. The taste of regret.

These days, tourists come. En route to somewhere else,
they stop for photos, stud the sand with gum.
Nothing to show the history here
but salt crust on the soles of their trainers.
A gold band, miles underneath,
is preserved like a beetle in amber.

Stargazing

Warm with beer, and a slew of humid hours
in a fug of people-heat, and breath, we leave the pub to stew
in cosy yellowness, and enter the black lane that leads to the tent.
The first corner swallows the light and muffled laughs we left behind,
and – that quick! – there is only blackness: sea-deep, soot-soft,
immediate. When darkness is this total, faith does not mean god,
but only your two feet testing again and again the firmament.
Trust does not mean belief, but only settled earth
being there, and there, and again, there. And up is sometimes down.
And there is sometimes not. And the stars are everywhere: in our hair
and underfoot, and in the sky, and in our pockets, and scattered in
the tree roots like rain, so only our linked arms stop us spinning
off the brink and into endless space, two wheels
of skin and bones, two wheels of dreams and teeth.

I saw it first, but it was on the tip of your finger that it danced –
that flaming, falling light, a line as clean as a cut. No words
for such a gift as that. We held each other. Breathed into the damp night.
The world was different, now. We had reinvented it.

Even The Skies
Iceland

Even the skies have language here.
Things must hatch in a land where even the clouds have mouths,
where rivers run space-green, gas-flame blue, taste joy, and return it,
like a just-ringed bride with *yes* in the flue of her throat.
Water freezes in rock-cracks, here; splits stone
with breakbone shrieks. Books part like that.
Like wild things under stars and teeth. Like continents
shuffled by tectonic plates. And afterwards, the world is altered,

the air is charged with the ghost of the last echo.
Words steam in this country. Blood hisses on snow.

Brooklyn

Sun-blessed skin after eight grey months: you step into the street,
turn on like a lamp. Your throat is touched with light,

and I see a child's chin, a flower's lifted cup;
the golden hum of honey in its jar. Your eyes are slits,

shut like the eyes of a stretching cat or
twinkling Buddha. Joy at its plainest.

I've seen that incandescence burn
in teenage girls, girls on the cusp.

The slim gleam of newly elongated legs. The grace
of small breasts in soft lace. But no-one, no-one

burns like you. Is half as golden.
Except perhaps me, when your eyes open,

and catch me in my own gold moment:
burning, watching you burn.

Long Grove

Imagine if you'd known in that first flush of fever
the time you'd endure in centimetres. The geological age
between Christmases. How *sick* would become *monochromatic*.

White. All white. Except for the scratched brass, and the green
that rises when they say *Make a fist*. And the blue eyes
above the white masks. You tell yourself

you cannot lose what you can still name, say *yellow* in earnest,
yellow, yellow. Later, *daughter*, into your pillow.
Your body - they repeat this - is now a bomb. You must keep

to paper slippers, a single room. They are afraid of bacteria.
You only of tedium. Once, you found a spider crouched in the sink,
and cried for the exquisite joy of something new.

Sometimes, you think you cannot bear
the weight of one stopped minute more. One single hour.
But then you do. And then you do.

*Note: Between 1944 and 1992, at least forty-three female typhoid carriers
were kept in a secure isolation unit at Long Grove Hospital in Surrey.
Despite having recovered from the disease, the women were deemed a public
health risk as they still hosted the bacteria, and were kept incarcerated on
this basis.*

Lluvia de Peces

You'll speak of it for years:
the day the fish fell, like stars or prayers,

a finned rain filling the sky with silver.
You'll say *phenomenon*. Say *miracle*. Say

fish out of water, which is how you felt
with your two feet sharing the same firmament.

Rainbows carving the air.
You never knew how many plates

held skydrowned bones that night,
could only guess from the smell

that swam through empty streets –
fat and seaspit greased with butter, dressed

with twists of lemon, salt – as though
each asphalt-dented swimmer

had risen from insult on a tide of steam
to breast again that current up

to cloud and star. Glutted with light.
Gravel-scarred. And in the air,

a hundred wakes as bright as comet-tails.
And on your hands, a scattering of scales.

Railway Station, Platform 2

The darkness wasn't darkness yet, but holding blue,
and it was simple movement I saw first, as though shadows
were accruing, the way a storm builds on nothing towards
being. Then the gold rings, like rings at a wedding,
shadow swearing to shadow. And then, from air, a fox rising
like a girl from water in a red dress. Or a bride, triumphant in lace,
her knuckle flashing, signalling *yes*. I can't be certain if I was breathing.
I can tell you a hummingbird broke out of my chest.

Prizes and Commendations

The Cartographer's Daughter was winner of the High Sheriff's Cheshire Prize for Literature 2016

Mam Tor won 3rd prize in Bare Fiction Poetry Competition 2015

Bat was shortlisted for York Literature Festival Poetry Competition 2013

Stargazing and *The Shape of Things* (previously *On Change*) were shortlisted for the Princemere Poetry Prize 2015

The Bearded Lady was nominated for a 2017 Pushcart Prize

Pre-Dawn was featured in The Guardian's Poetry Workshop